LITTLE HENRY AND HIS BEARER

LITTLE HENRY

AND

HIS BEARER

A TALE OF DINAPORE

BY

MARY M. SHERWOOD

THE AUTHOR OF "THE LITTLE WOODMAN."

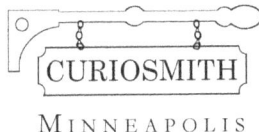

CURIOSMITH

MINNEAPOLIS

Published by Curiosmith.
P. O. Box 390293, Minneapolis, Minnesota, 55439.
Internet: curiosmith.com.
E-mail: shopkeeper@curiosmith.com.

Previously published by F. HOULSTON AND SON in 1814.

Scripture verses are from *The Holy Bible*, King James Version.

ISBN 9781935626886

CONTENTS

LITTLE HENRY AND HIS BEARER
A Tale of Dinapore

Henry L—— was born at Dinapore in the East Indies. His father was an officer in the Company's service, and was killed in attacking a mud fort belonging to a petty *Zemeendar*,[1] a few months after the birth of his son. His mother also died before he was a year old. Thus little Henry was left an orphan when he was a very little baby; but his dying mother, when taking her last farewell of him, lifted up her eyes to heaven, and said, "O God, I leave my fatherless child with thee, claiming thy promise in all humility, yet in full confidence that my baby will never be left destitute; for in thee the fatherless find mercy." The promise to which she alluded is to be found in Jeremiah 49:11. "Leave thy fatherless children, I will preserve them alive; and let thy widows trust in me."

As soon as Henry's mamma was dead, a lady, who lived at that time in a large *puckah*[2] house near the river between Patna and Dinapore, came and took little Henry, and gave him a room in her house, giving strict orders to her servants to provide him with everything that he wanted. But as she was one of those fine ladies who will give their money (when they have any to spare)

---

1 Zemeendar—a landowner.
2 Puckah—brick or stone.

for the relief of distress, but have no idea how it is possible for any one to bestow all his goods to feed the poor, and yet want *charity;* she thought that when she had received the child, and given her orders to her servants, she had done all that was necessary for him. She would not afterwards suffer Henry to give her the least trouble, nor would she endure the smallest inconvenience on his account; and thus the poor child, being very small and unable to make known his wants, might have been cruelly neglected, had it not been for the attention of a *bearer,*[1] who had lived many years with his papa, and had taken care of Henry from the day that he was born.

When he was a very little baby, Boosy (for that was the bearer's name) attended him night and day, warmed his pap, rocked his cot, dressed and undressed and washed him, and did everything for him as tenderly as if he had been his own child. The first word that little Henry tried to say, was *Boosy;* and when he was only ten months old he used to put his arms round his neck and kiss him, or stroke his swarthy cheek with his little delicate hand.

When Henry was carried to the lady's house, Boosy went with him; and for some years the little child had no other friend than his *bearer.* Boosy never left his *choota sahib,*[2] except for two hours in the twenty-four, when he went to get his *khauna.*[3] At night he slept on his mat at the foot of the child's cot; and whenever Henry called, he was up in a moment, and had milk or toast-and-water ready to give him to drink. Early in the morning, before sunrise, he took him out in a little carriage which was provided for him, or carried him in his arms around the garden.

1 Bearer—a servant whose work it is to assist in carrying a palanquin, in which persons in India ride, as in a carriage; but who is frequently employed to take care of children.
2 Choota sahib—little master.
3 Khauna—food.

When he brought him in, he bathed him and dressed him, and gave him his breakfast, and put him in his cot to sleep: and all the day long he played with him; sometimes carrying him in his arms, or on his back, and sometimes letting him walk, or roll upon the carpet. Every body who came to the house noticed the kindness of Boosy to the child, and he got presents from many people for his goodness to Henry.

When Henry was two years old he had a dreadful illness; so alarming indeed was it, that for many days it was thought he would die. He had afterwards a very severe illness when he was four years old, for he was never a very healthy child. During the height of these sicknesses his *bearer* never left him; nor would he take any rest, even by the side of his bed, till he thought the danger was over.

These things considered, it cannot be a matter of wonder that this little boy, as he grew older, should love his bearer more than all the world besides; for his *bearer* was almost his only friend, no one else taking any thought about him. Henry could not speak English, but he could talk with Boosy in *his* language as fast as possible; and he knew every word, good or bad, which the natives spoke. He used to sit in the *varandah*[1] between his *bearer's* knees and chew *paun*[2] and eat *bazar*[3] sweetmeats. He wore no shoes nor stockings; but was dressed in *pangammahs*,[4] and had silver *bangles*[5] on his ankles. No one could have told by his behavior or manner of speaking that he was not of Indian origin; but his delicate complexion, light hair, and blue eyes at once showed his parentage.

---

1 Verandah—an open gallery or passage.
2 Paun—an intoxicating mixture of opium and sugar, etc.
3 Bazar—a market.
4 Pangammahs—trousers.
5 Bangles—ornaments generally worn round the wrists and ankles.

All the day long he played with him; sometimes carrying him in his arms or on his shoulder, and sometimes letting him walk, or roll upon the carpet. Everybody who came to the house noticed the kindness of Boosy to the child.

Thus his life passed till he was five years and a half old: for the lady in whose house he lived (although he was taught to call her mamma) paid him no kind of attention; and it never occurred to her that it was her duty to give him any religious instructions. He used to see his *bearer* and the other natives performing *poojah*,[1] and carrying about their wooden and clay gods; and he knew that his mamma sometimes went to church at Dinapore: so he believed that there were a great many gods, and that the God that his mamma went to pray to at Dinapore was no better than the gods of wood, and stone, and clay which his *bearer* worshipped. He also believed that the River Ganges was a goddess, called Gunga; and that the water of the river would take away sins. He believed, too, that the *Mussulmans*[2] were as good as Christians, for his mamma's *khaunsaumaun*[3] had told him so. Besides these, he was taught by the servants many other things which a little boy should not know: but the servants, being heathen, could not be expected to teach him any thing better; and therefore they were not so much to be blamed as the lady who had undertaken the charge of Henry, who might have been ashamed to leave the child of Christian parents under the care of such persons.

When Henry was five years old, a young lady, who was just arrived from England, came to reside for a while with his mamma. She was the daughter of a worthy clergyman in England, and had received from him a religious education. She had brought with her from home a box of Bibles, and some pretty little children's books and pictures. When she saw poor little Henry sitting in the *verandah*, as his custom was, between his *bearer's* knees, with many other native servants surrounding

---

1 Poojah—ceremony or offering.
2 Mussulmans—Muslims.
3 Khaunsaumaun—a kind of house-steward.

him, she loved him, and was very sorry for him; for indeed, it is a dreadful thing for little children to be left among people who know not God. So she took some of the prettiest colored pictures she had and spread them on the floor of the room, the door of which happened to open into the *verandah* near the place where the little boy usually sat. When Henry peeped in and saw the pictures, he was tempted by them to come into the room; but at first he would not venture in without his *bearer*. Afterwards, when he got more accustomed to the lady, he was contented that his *bearer* should sit at the door while he went in. And at last he quite lost all fear, and would go in by himself: nay, he never was more happy than when he was with this lady; for she tried every means to gain his love, in order that she might lead him to receive such instructions as the time of her intended stay with his mamma would allow her to give him.

She was very sorry when she found that he could not speak English; however, she was resolved not to be checked by this difficulty. She taught him many English words by showing him things represented in the colored pictures, telling him their English names; so that in a short time he could ask for anything he wanted in English. She then taught him his letters in one of the little books she had brought from home, and from his letters she proceeded to spelling: and so diligent was she, that before he was six years old he could spell any words, however difficult, and could speak English quite readily.

While this young lady was taking pains, from day to day, to teach little Henry to read, she endeavored by word of mouth to make him acquainted with such parts of the Christian religion as even the youngest ought to know; and without the knowledge of which no one can be a Christian; and she did not like to wait until Henry could read his Bible, before she would instruct him in subjects of so much importance.

The first lesson of this kind which she strove to teach him, was, that there was only *one true God*, and that he made all things, namely, the glorious heaven, to which those persons go who have been made the children of God on earth; and the dreadful hell, prepared for those who die in their sins; the world, and all things in it; the sun, the moon, the stars, and all the heavenly bodies. And she was going to teach him the following words from Colossians 1:16: "For by him were all things created, that are in heaven and that are in earth"—but no sooner did little Henry understand that she meant to teach him that there is but one God, than he got very angry, and told her that she did not speak a *true word;* for his mamma had a God, and his *bearer* had a god, and there were a great many gods: and he ran out into the *verandah* and told his *bearer* what the *chootee bebee*[1] had said; and he sat down between his *bearer's* knees, and would not come to her again that day, although she brought out her finest pictures and a new book, on purpose to tempt him.

The young lady did not fail to pray very earnestly for little Henry that night, when she was withdrawn to her room, and her door shut. And her Father, on whom she called in secret, in the name of his beloved Son, heard her prayer: for the next day little Henry came smiling into the room, having quite forgotten his fit of ill-humor; and she was now enabled to talk to him with advantage on the same subject. And she made him kneel down, and pray to God to give him sense to understand the truth. She had also provided herself with one of the *Hindoo*[2] gods made of baked earth; and she bade him look at it, and examine it well: she then threw it down upon the floor, and it was broken into an hundred pieces. Then she said, "Henry, what can this god do

1 Chootee bebee—young lady.
2 Hindoo—Hindu.

for you? it cannot help itself. Call to it, and ask it to get up. You see it cannot move."—And that day the little boy was convinced by her arguments.

The next discourse which the young lady had with Henry was upon the nature of God. She taught him that God is a spirit; that he is everywhere; that he can do everything; that he can see everything; that he can hear everything; that he knows even the inmost thoughts of our hearts; that he loves that which is good, and hates that which is evil; that he never had a beginning, and never will have an end. She also taught him, that in this one and only true God there are three persons, namely, God the Father, God the Son, and God the Holy Ghost: and that these three Persons, although none is afore or after the other, perform different works or offices for man.

Henry now began to take pleasure in hearing of God, and asked many questions about him. He next learned that God made the world in six days, and rested from his work on the seventh and that he made man and woman innocent at first. He then was taught how our forefather Adam was tempted, with Eve his wife, to eat the forbidden fruit: and how by this means sin entering into the world, and the nature of Adam becoming sinful, all we his children, being born in his likeness, are sinful also.

Henry here asked what sin is?

"Sin, my child," answered the lady, "is whatever displeases God. If your mamma were to desire you to come into her room, or to do something for her, and you were to refuse, would she not have reason to be displeased with you?"

"Yes, I suppose so."

"Or if you ask Boosy to fan you, or to carry you in your palanquin, and Boosy does something quite different; or if you desire him to carry you one way, and he carries you another; would he not do wrong?"

"Yes, to be sure."

"Well, then; whatever you do contrary to the commands of God displeases him, and is sin."

But the lady still found great difficulty in making Henry understand the nature of sin: for he had been so neglected that he did not know right from wrong. He did not consider a lie as sinful; nor feel ashamed of stealing, unless it was found out. He thought, also, that if any body hurt him, it was right to hurt them in return. After several days, however, she made the subject clear to him; and then further explained how sin has corrupted all our hearts: and she made him repeat the following words till he could say them quite well: "The Lord looked down from heaven upon the children of men, to see if there were any that did understand, and seek God. They are all gone aside, they are altogether become filthy; there is none that doeth good, no, not one." Psalm 14:2–3.

She next made the little boy understand that eternal death, or everlasting punishment, is the consequence of sin; and he soon could repeat two or three verses to prove this: one was, "The unrighteous shall not inherit the kingdom of God;" 1 Corinthians 6:9; and another, "They shall look upon the carcasses of the men that have transgressed against me; for their worm shall not die, neither shall their fire be quenched; and they shall be an abhorring unto all flesh." Isaiah 66:24.

And now the lady had brought Henry to know that he and all the world were sinners, and that the punishment of sin is eternal death; and that it was not in his power to save himself, nor of any thing on the earth to wash him from his sins; and she had brought him several times to ask her with great earnestness what he must do to be saved, and how his sins could be forgiven, and his heart freed from evil tempers—her next lesson, therefore, was to explain to him what the Lord Jesus Christ had done for him; how "God was manifest in the flesh, justified in the Spirit, seen of angels, preached unto the Gentiles, believed on in the world, received up into glory;" 1 Timothy 3:16; and how "we have redemption through his blood," he "having made peace for us through the blood of his cross." Colossians 1:14, 20.

Little Henry was particularly pleased whenever he heard of our Savior: and, by divine grace, his heart seemed to be wonderfully filled with love for his Redeemer; and he was so afraid of offending him, that he became careful of every word he said and of every thing he did; and he was always asking the young lady if *this* was right? and if *that* was right? and if God would be angry with him if he did *this* or *that?* so that in a short time his whole behavior was altered. He never said a bad word, and was vexed when he heard any other person do it. He spoke mildly and civilly to everybody. He would return the *salam*[1] of the poorest *coolie*[2] in the market. If any body had given him a *rupee*,[3] he would not spend it in sweetmeats or playthings; but he would change it into *pice*[4] and give it to the *fakeers*[5] who were blind or lame, or such as seemed to be in real distress, as far as it would go.

One day Henry came into the lady's room, and found her opening a box of books. "Come," said she, "Henry, help me unpack these books, and to carry them to my bookcase." Now, while they were thus busy, and little Henry much pleased to think that he could make himself useful, the lady said, "These books have different kinds of covers, and some are larger than others, but they all contain the same words, and are the book of God. If you read this book, and with God's help, keep the

---

1 Salam—health; salutation.
2 Coolie—a kind of low cast of men, who have no trade, but work at any kind of common employment.
3 Rupee—a silver coin of the value of half-a-crown.
4 Pice—pence.
5 Fakeers—a religious order of men, something like monks or dervises.

sayings written in it, it will bring you to heaven; it will bring you to where your beloved Redeemer is; to the throne of the Lamb of God, who was slain for your sins."

"O! I wish," said Henry, "that I had one of these books! I will give you all my playthings, ma'am, and my little carriage, for one of them."

The lady smiled, and said, "No, my dear, keep your playthings, and your little carriage too: you shall have any one of these books you like best."

Henry thanked the lady with all his heart, and called Boosy in to give his advice whether he should choose a book with a purple morocco cover, or one with a red one. When he had fixed upon one, he begged a bit of silk of the lady, and carried it to the tailor to make him a bag for his new Bible: and that same evening he came to the lady to beg her to teach him to read it.

So that day he began: and he was several days over the first chapter of Genesis; but the next chapter was easier, and the next easier still; till very soon he was able to read any part of the Bible without hesitation.

With what joy and gratitude to God did the young lady see the effects of her pious labors! She had in the space of a year and a half, brought a little orphan from the grossest state of heathen darkness and ignorance to a competent knowledge of those doctrines of the Christian religion which are chiefly necessary to salvation. She had put into his hand the book of God, and had taught him to read it; and God had, in an especial manner, answered all her prayers for the dear child.

The time was now coming on very fast when she must leave little Henry; and the thoughts of this parting were very painful to her. Some days before she set out on her journey, she called him into her room, and questioned him concerning the things which she had taught him; directing him, as often as he could, to give his answers from the Bible. Her first question was, "How many Gods are there?"

HENRY. "There is one God; and there is none other but he." Mark 12:32.

LADY. Do we not believe that there are three Persons in this one God?

HENRY. "There are three that bear record in heaven; the Father, the Word, and the Holy Ghost; and these three are one." 1 John 5:7.

LADY. What do you mean by the Word?

HENRY. The Word is the Lord Jesus Christ.

LADY. Do you know that from the Bible?

HENRY. Yes; for St. John says, in the first chapter of his Gospel, "In the beginning was the Word, and the Word was with God, and the Word was God. He was in the world, and the world was made by him, and the world knew him not."[1]

LADY. Did God make man good at first?

HENRY. Yes; for in the first chapter of the Bible, the last verse, it is written, "God saw every thing that he had made, and behold, it was very good."[2]

LADY. Are men very good now? Can you find me one person who deserves to be called good?

HENRY. I need not look into the Bible to answer that question. I need but just get into the *palanquin*, and go into the market, and show you the people there: I am sure I could not find one good person in the market.

LADY. But I think, Henry, you might spare yourself the trouble of going into the market to see how bad human creatures are; could you not find proofs of that nearer home?

HENRY. What, our servants you mean? Or, perhaps, the

---

1 John 1:1, 10.
2 Genesis 1:31.

ladies in the hall with my mamma? They laughed at the Bible at breakfast; I knew what they meant very well; and my mamma laughed too: I am sure nobody can say that they are good.

LADY. No, my dear; those poor ladies are not good: it would be misleading you to say they are. But as we cannot make them better by speaking ill of them in their absence, it would be better not to mention them at all, unless it were in prayer to God that he would turn their hearts. But to return to my question—You need not go so far as the hall for an answer to it. There is a little boy in this very room, called Henry: can he be said to be a good boy? A very few months ago that little boy used to tell lies every day; and only yesterday I saw him in a passion, because the *sais*[1] would not let him get on the back of one of the coach-horses; and I think, but I am not sure, that he gave the coachman a blow with his hand.

HENRY. I know it was very wicked: but I had no stick in my hand, and therefore I hope I did not hurt him. I hope God will give me grace never to do so again. I gave the *sais* all that I had left of my *rupee* this morning; and I told him I was very sorry.

LADY. I mentioned it, my dear, that you might know where to look for an answer to my question.

HENRY. Oh! I know that I am not good. I have done many, many naughty things, which nobody knows of; no, not even Boosy. And God only can know the naughtiness of my heart.

LADY. Then you think yourself a great sinner?

HENRY. A very great one.

LADY. Where do sinners go when they die?

HENRY. "The wicked shall be turned into hell, and all the nations that forget God." Psalm 9:17.

LADY. If all the wicked people are turned into hell, how can you escape?

---

1 Sais—a servant who has the charge of a horse.

HENRY. If I believe on the Lord Jesus Christ, I shall be saved. Stay one moment and I will show the verse. "Believe on the Lord Jesus Christ and thou shalt be saved." Acts 16:31.

LADY. What! if you believe in the Lord Jesus Christ, shall you go to heaven with all your sins? Can sinful creatures be in heaven?

HENRY. No; to be sure not. God cannot live with sinners. He is, "of purer eyes than to behold evil." Habakkuk 1:13. But if I believe in the Lord Jesus Christ, he will take away my sin; for his "blood cleanseth from all sin;" 1 John 1:7; and he will give me a new heart, and make me a new creature, and I shall purify myself, as he is pure. 1 John 3:3.

Now the lady was pleased with little Henry's answers: and she thanked God in her heart for having so blessed her labors with the poor little boy. But she did not praise him, lest he should become proud: and she well knew that "God resisteth the proud, but giveth grace to the humble." James 4:6. So she refrained from commending him; but she said, "What do you mean, my dear, by being made quite new again?"

HENRY. Before I knew the Lord Jesus Christ, I used to think of nothing but naughty things. I loved myself more than anybody else. I loved eating fruit and sweetmeats; and was so greedy of them that I would have told a hundred lies, I do think, for one mouthful of them. Then I was passionate and proud. I used to be so pleased when any body bowed to me, and said, *"Sahib."* And you cannot think how cruel I was to all kinds of little creatures I could get hold of, even the poor cock-roaches: I used to kill them just for my own pleasure. But now I do think my heart is beginning to change a little, I mean a very little, for I gave all my last sweetmeats to the *matre's*[1] boy. But still I know that my heart is far from being clean yet; but God

1 Matre—a sweeper: a person of low caste, who eats everything.

can make it white and clean when he pleases.

LADY. You must pray every day, and oftentimes in the day; and in the night, when you are awake, my dear child; that God will send his Holy Spirit into your heart, to make it clean and pure, and to lead and direct you in all you do. Blessed are those, my dear child, who love the Lord Jesus Christ: for unto them "the Spirit of truth" shall be revealed; and it "shall dwell with them, and be in them." John 14:17.

She then shut the door of the room; and she and the little boy knelt down together, and prayed to God, that he would, for his dear Son's sake, "create a clean heart" in the child, "and renew a right spirit within" him. Psalm 51:10. When the young lady arose from her knees, she kissed little Henry, and told him, not without many tears, that she must soon go away from him.

When Henry heard this news, for some moments he could not speak; at length he cried out, "What shall I do when you are gone! I shall have nobody to speak to but my *bearer,* for my mamma does not love me; and I shall spend all my time with the natives. I shall never more hear any body talk of God. Oh! I very much fear that I shall become wicked again."

"My poor child," said the lady, "do not doubt the power of God. When our Savior was going to leave his disciples, he said, 'I will not leave you orphans;[1] I will come to you.' John 14:18. And do you think, my child, that after the blessed Lord God has made himself known unto you as a dear son, he will leave you comfortless? Think how good he was to call you from the paths of destruction, and from the way of hell. You knew not so much as his holy name, and were living altogether among the Heathen. It was by his providence that I came here; that I remained here so long that I loved you, and endeavored to teach you; and that I had a Bible to give you. 'Faithful is he,'

1 The word is orphans in the original.

my beloved child, 'who called you. He will preserve your whole spirit and soul and body blameless unto the coming of the Lord Jesus.'" 1 Thessalonians 5:23–24. She then sung a verse of a hymn to him; which he often repeated, and would try to sing when she was far away from him.

> "Jesus sought me when a stranger,
>   Wandering from the fold of God;
> He, to save my soul from danger,
>   Interposed his precious blood."[1]

Now it would take more time than I have to spare, to repeat the several conversations which this young lady had with little Henry before she went away. He cried sadly the day she went. He followed her down to the river-side; for she was going to Berhampore, where she was soon afterwards married to a very pious young man of the name of Baron.

Henry went on board the *budgerow*,[2] to take leave of her. She kissed him many times before they parted; and gave Boosy, who was with him, four *rupees, buckshish,* that he might continue to behave well to his *sahib.* The last words almost that she said to Henry were these, "You must try, my dear child, with the grace of God, to make Boosy a Christian; that he may be no longer numbered among the Heathen, but may be counted among the sons of God."

When the *budgerow* was ready to sail, little Henry took his last leave of the lady, and came on shore; where he stood under the shade of a *Braminee fig-tree*,[3] watching the boat as it sailed

---

1 *Come Thou Fount of Every Blessing* by Robert Robinson, sung to the tune of the Sicilian Mariner's Hymn.
2 Budgerow—a kind of barge.
3 Braminee fig-tree—a tree, that takes root downward from its branches.

down the broad stream of the Ganges, till it was hidden by the winding shore. Then Boosy, taking him up in his arms, brought him back to his mamma's house: and from that time he was as much neglected as he had been before this good young lady came; with this difference only, (and that indeed was a blessing for which I doubt not he will thank God to all eternity,) that he was now able to read the book of God; whereas, before, he knew not even God's holy name.

Sometimes his mamma would let him eat his *tiffin*[1] with her; but, as she always employed herself at table (when not actually eating) in smoking her *hookah,*[2] and as most of her visitors did the same, the *tiffin* time was very stupid to the little boy; for, instead of pleasant and useful discourse, there was in general nothing to be heard at these meals but the rattling of plates and knives and forks, the creaking of the *punkah*[3] suspended from the ceiling; and the guggling of water in the *hookah;* except his mamma (which not unseldom happened) occasioned a little variety by scolding the servants, and calling them names in their own language.

So poor little Henry found no better companion than his *bearer;* and he never was more pleased than when he was sitting by him in the *verandah*, reading his Bible to himself.

And now the young lady's last words returned to his mind, namely, "You must try to make Boosy a Christian." But he did not know how to begin this work: it seemed to him, that the heart of poor Boosy could only be changed by the immediate interference of God; so fond was he of his wooden gods and foolish ceremonies, and so much was he afraid of offending his

1 Tiffin—luncheon.
2 Hookah—a kind of pipe, the smoke of which is drawn through water, and the motion of the air through the water causes a bubbling noise.
3 Punkah—a large fan suspended from the ceiling.

gooroo.[1] And in this respect Henry judged rightly; for no one can come to God without the help of God; yet he has pointed out the means by which we must endeavor to bring our fellow-creatures to him; and we must, in faith and humility, use these means, praying for the divine blessing to render them effectual.

The first step which Henry took towards this work, was to pray for Boosy. After some thought he made a prayer, which was much to this purpose: "O Lord God, hear the humble prayer of a poor little sinful child. Give me power, O God, for thy dear Son's sake, who died for us upon the cross, to turn the heart of my poor *bearer* from his wooden gods, and to lead him to the cross of Jesus Christ." This prayer he never failed to repeat every night, and many times a day: and from time to time he used to talk to Boosy, and repeat to him many things which the young lady had taught him. But although Boosy heard him with good humor, yet he did not seem to pay much heed to what the child said; for he would argue to this purpose: "There are many brooks and rivers of water, but they all run into the sea at last; so there are a great many religions, but they all lead to heaven: there is the Mussulmaun's way to heaven, and the Hindoo's way, and the Christian's way: and one way is as good as another." He asserted also, that if he were to commit the greatest sin, and were to go immediately afterwards and wash in the Ganges, he should be quite innocent. And a great many other foolish things he had to say to the same purpose, so that he sometimes quite out-talked the child. But Henry was so earnest in the cause he had undertaken, that although he might be silenced at one time, yet he would often, after having said his prayer and consulted his Bible, begin the attack again. He would sometimes get close to him, and look in his face, and say, "Poor Boosy! Poor Boosy! you are going the wrong way, and will not let me set you

1 Gooroo—a religious teacher, or confessor.

right: there is but one way to heaven; our Savior, the Lord Jesus Christ, is *the way* to heaven, and 'no man cometh unto God but by him.'" John 14:6. Then he would try to explain who the Lord Jesus Christ is: how he came down to the earth; that he took man's nature upon him; suffered and died upon the cross for the sins of men; was buried and rose again on the third day, and ascended into heaven; and is now sitting at the right hand of God, from whence he will come to judge the quick and the dead.

In this manner the little boy proceeded from day to day, but Boosy seemed to pay him little or no attention; nay, he would sometimes laugh at him, and ask him why he was so earnest about a thing of so little consequence! However, to do Boosy justice, he never was ill-humored or disrespectful to his little *sahib*.

Now it happened, about this time, that Henry's mamma had occasion to go to Calcutta; and, as she went by water, she took Henry and his *bearer* in the *budgerow* with her. Henry had not been well, and she thought the change of air might do him good. It was at the end of the rains; at that season of the year when India is most green and beautiful, although not most healthy. When the *budgerow* came to anchor in the evening, Henry used to take a walk with his *bearer;* and sometimes they would ramble among the fields and villages for more than a mile from the river. Henry had all his life been confined to one spot; so, you may be sure, he was well pleased to see so many different countries, and asked many questions about the things which he saw. And often, during these rambles he used to have an argument with Boosy concerning the great Creator of all things: and Henry would say to his *bearer*, that the great God, who made all things, could not be like the gods which he believed in, which, according to his accounts of them, were more wicked and foolish than the worst men.

Once, in particular—it was in one of those lovely places near the *Raja-mehal*[1] hills—Henry and his *bearer* went to walk. Henry's mamma had during the day been very cross to him, and the poor little fellow did not feel well, although he did not complain; but he was glad when he got out of the boat. The sun was just setting, and a cool breeze blew over the water, with which the little boy, being refreshed, climbed without difficulty to the top of a little hill where was a tomb. Here they sat down: and Henry could not but admire the beautiful prospect which was before them. On their left hand was the broad stream of the Ganges, winding round the curved shore, till it was lost behind the Raja-mehal hills. The *budgerow*, gaily painted, anchored just below them, and with it many smaller boats, with thatched and sloping roofs. The *dandies*[2] and native servants, having finished their day's work, were preparing their *khauna*, in distinct parties, according to their several *casts*,[3] upon the banks of the river; some grinding their *mussala*,[4] some lighting their little fires, some washing their brass vessels, and others sitting in a circle upon the ground smoking their cocoa-nut *hookahs*. Before them, on the right hand, was a beautiful country abounding with corn-fields, *topes* of trees, thatched cottages, with their little bamboo porches, plantain, and palm-trees; beyond which the *Raja-mehal* hills were seen, some bare to their summits, and others covered with *jungle*,[5] which even now afford a shelter to tigers, rhinoceroses, and wild hogs.

Henry sat silent a long time. At last he said, "Boosy, this is a good country: that is, it would be a very good country if the people were Christians. Then they would not be so idle as they

1 Raja-mehal—the hall of the rajah.
2 Dandies—boatman.
3 Cast—a class of the same rank.
4 Mussala—a general name for spices, salt, medicine, etc.
5 Jungle—uncultivated waste land, overrun with brushwood or reeds.

now are; and they would agree together, and clear the *jungles*, and build churches to worship God in. It will be pleasant to see the people, when they are Christians, all going on a Sabbath morning to some pretty church, built among those hills, and to see them in an evening sitting at the door of their houses reading the *shaster*[1]—I do not mean *your* shaster, but *our* shaster—God's book."

Boosy answered, that he knew there would be a time when all the world would be of one religion, and when there would be no cast; but he did not know when that would be, and he was sure he should not live to see it.

"There is a country now," said Henry, "where there are no *casts;* and where we all shall be like dear brothers. It is a better country than this; there are no evil beasts; there is no more hunger, no more thirst; there the waters are sure; there the sun does not scorch by day, nor the moon smite by night. It is a country to which I sometimes think and hope I shall go very soon; I wish, Boosy, you would be persuaded either to go with me, or to follow me."

"What!" said Boosy, "is *sahib* going to *Willaet?*"[2] And then he said he hoped not; for he could never follow him through the black water, as the Hindoos call the seas.

Henry then explained to him, that he did not mean England, but heaven. "Sometimes I think," said he, "when I feel the pain which I did this morning, that I shall not live long; I think I shall die soon, Boosy. O, I wish! I wish I could persuade you to love the Lord Jesus Christ!" And then Henry, getting up, threw his arms around Boosy's neck, and begged him to be a Christian. "Dear Boosy," said he, "good Boosy, do try to be a Christian." But poor little Henry's attempts were yet quite ineffectual.

1 Shaster—the Hindoo religious books.
2 Willaet—country; but generally applied to Europe.

In little more than a month's time from their leaving Dinapore they reached Calcutta, and were received into the house of a worthy gentleman of the name of Smith.

When Henry's mamma was settled in Mr. Smith's house she found less inclination, if possible, than ever, to pay any attention to Henry. According to the custom of India, she must pay the first visit to all her acquaintance in Calcutta. Her dresses, too, having all been made at Dinapore, did not agree with the last European fashions which were come out: these were all to be altered, and new ones bought; and it was a good deal of trouble to direct the tailor to do this properly. Her hair was not dressed in the fashion: and her *ayah*[1] was very stupid; it was many days before she could forget the old way and learn the new way. So poor Henry was quite forgotten in all this bustle; and although he was for several days very ill, and complained to his *bearer* that his side gave him great pain his mamma never knew it.

Mr. and Mrs. Smith once or twice remarked, when they looked at Henry, that the child was very pale, and that his eyes were heavy: but his mamma answered, "O, this is nothing; the child is well enough; children in India, you know, have that look."

It happened one afternoon, as Mr. and Mrs. Smith and Henry's mamma were in the drawing room after *tiffin*, while the ladies were giving their opinion upon a magazine which contained an account of the last European fashion of carriages and dresses, etc. (for I am sorry to say that Mrs. Smith, although she had the best example in her husband, had still to learn not to love the world,) Mr. Smith, half angry with them, and yet not knowing whether he should presume to give them a check, was walking up and down the room with rather a hasty step; when his eye, as he passed the door, caught little Henry sitting on the mat at the

1 Ajah—a waiting-maid.

head of the stairs, between his *bearer's* knees, with his Bible in his hand. His back being turn towards the drawing-room door, Mr. Smith had an opportunity of observing what he was about, without being seen: he accordingly stood still, and listened: and he heard the gentle voice of Henry, as he tried to interpret the sacred book to his *bearer* in the *bearer's* own language!

Mr. Smith at first could scarcely believe what he saw and heard; but, at last, being quite sure he was not dreaming, he turned hastily towards the ladies, exclaiming, "Twenty-five years have I been in India, and never have I seen any thing like this. Heaven be praised! truly it is written, 'Out of the mouths of babes and sucklings thou hast perfected praise.' Matthew 21:16. For shame, for shame! Mrs. Smith, will you never lay aside your toys and gewgaws? Do give me that book, and I will let the cook have it to light his fire with.—Here are two persons, who have been nearly fifty years in the world, sitting together talking of their finery and painted toys; while a little creature, who eight years ago had not breathed the breath of life, is endeavoring to impart divine knowledge to the heathen. 'But God hath chosen the foolish things of the world to confound the wise; and God hath chosen the weak things of the world to confound the things which are mighty.'" 1 Corinthians 1:27.

"My dear," cried Mrs. Smith, "surely you forget yourself! What can you mean?—Toys and finery,—my dear, my dear, you are very rude!"

"Rude!" said Henry's mamma, "rude indeed! Mr. Smith—and pray, sir, what do you mean by saying 'Fifty years?' Do you suppose that I am fifty years old?—Extraordinary indeed!"

"I beg pardon," said Mr. Smith, "I did not mean to offend—but there is that little boy trying to explain the Bible to his *bearer*."

"But, surely," said Henry's mamma, "you do not think that I

am fifty years of age?—you are mistaken by twenty years."

MRS. SMITH. O! my dear madam, you must excuse my husband—Whenever he is a little angry with me, he tells me that I am getting old. But I am so used to it that I never mind it.

MR. SMITH. Well, my dear; leave me, if you please, to speak for myself. I am not a man that disguises the truth. Whether I speak or not, time runs on, death and eternity approach. I do not see why it should be a matter of politeness to throw dust in each other's eyes.—But enough of this, and too much. I want to know the meaning of what I but now saw; a little English child, seven years of age, endeavoring to explain the Bible to his *bearer*. I did not even know that the child could read.

"O," said Henry's mamma, "this matter is easily explained. I had a young lady at my house at Patna, some time since, who taught the child to read: for this I was obliged to her. But she was not satisfied with that alone; she made him an enthusiast, a downright canting enthusiast of the boy. I never knew it till it was too late."

MR. SMITH. An enthusiast! What do you mean, madam?

"Indeed," said Henry's mamma, "the child has never been himself since. Captain D—— of the —— native infantry, when they were quartered at Dinapore, used to have such sport with him! He taught him, when he was but two years old, to call the dogs and the horses, and to swear at the servants in English—but I shall offend Mr. Smith again," she added: "I suspect him a little of being a religious enthusiast himself. Am I right, Mrs. Smith?" and she laughed at her own wit. But Mrs. Smith looked grave; and Mr. Smith lifted up his eyes to heaven, saying, "May God Almighty turn your heart!"

"O, Mr. Smith," said Henry's mamma, "you take the matter too seriously: I was only speaking in jest."

"I shall put that to the trial, madam," said Mr. Smith. "If you

really feel no ill-will against religion, and people who call them-
selves religious, you will not refuse to let me consider Henry as
my pupil while you remain in my house, which I hope will be as
long as you can make it convenient. You have known me some
years, (I will not say how many, lest you should be angry again,)
and you will make allowances for my plain dealing."

"Well," said Henry's mamma, "we know you are an oddity;
take your own way, and let me take mine." So she got up to
dress for the evening airing on the course: and thus this strange
conversation ended in good humor; for she was not, upon the
whole, an ill-tempered woman.

The same evening, his mamma being gone out, Mr. Smith
called Henry into his own room, and learned from him all that
he could tell of his own history, and of the young lady who
taught him to read his Bible, and had advised him to try to
make Boosy a Christian. I will relate to you the last part of this
discourse which passed between Mr. Smith and Henry.

MR. SMITH. Do you think that Boosy's heart is at all turned
toward God?

HENRY. No, I do not think that it is; although for the last
half year I have been constantly talking to him about God; but
he still will have it that his own idols are true gods.

MR. SMITH. It is almost dangerous, my dear little boy, for
a child like you to dispute with a heathen: for although you are
in the right, and he in the wrong, yet Satan, who is the father
of lies, may put words into his mouth which may puzzle you;
so that your faith may be shaken, while his remains unchanged.

HENRY. Oh! sir, must I give up the hope of Boosy's being
made a Christian? Poor Boosy! he has taken care of me ever
since I was born.

MR. SMITH. But suppose, my dear boy, that I could put you
in a better way of converting Boosy: a safe way to yourself, and

a better for him? Can Boosy read?

HENRY. Only a very little, I believe.

MR. SMITH. Then you must learn to read for him.

HENRY. How, sir?

MR. SMITH. If I could get for you some of the most important chapters in the Bible, such as the first chapters of Genesis, which speak of the creation of the world and the fall of man, with the first promise of the Savior, and some parts of the Gospel, translated into Boosy's language, would you try to learn to read them to him? I will teach you the letters, or characters as they are called, in which they will be written.

HENRY. O! I will learn them with joy.

MR. SMITH. Well, my boy; come every morning into my study, and I will teach you the Persian characters; for those are what will be used in the copy of the chapters I shall put into your hands. Sometime or other the whole Bible will be translated in this manner.

HENRY. Will the words be Persian, sir? I know Boosy does not understand Persian.

MR. SMITH. No, my dear; the words will be the same as those you speak every day with the natives. When you have as much of the Bible as I can get prepared for you in this manner, you must read it to your *bearer* every day, praying continually, that God will bless his holy word to him. And never fear, my dear, but that the word of God will do its work; "for as the rain cometh down, and the snow from heaven, and returneth not thither, but watereth the earth, and maketh it bring forth and bud, that it may give seed to the sower, and bread to the eater; so shall my word be that goeth forth out of my mouth: it shall not return unto me void; but it shall accomplish that which I please, and it shall prosper in the thing whereto I sent it." Isaiah 55:10–11. "But do not, my dear boy," added Mr. Smith, "argue and dispute with your *bearer* about religion; you are not able. Only read the Bible to him, and pray for him continually; leaving the rest with God."

But not to make my story too long; while Henry's mamma remained at Calcutta, which was more than a year, Henry received a lesson every day from Mr. Smith in his study; and Mr. Smith taught him the Persian characters, and provided him with so many chapters in the Bible in Hindostannee as he could get properly prepared in so short a time: these he had bound in red morocco, and presented them to Henry, not without asking the blessing of God upon them.

How delighted was Henry when he received the book, and found that he could read it easily! He was in his place on the mat between Boosy's knees in a minute, and you might have heard him reading from one end of the house to the other, for he could not contain himself for joy. Nor was he contented with reading himself, he must make Boosy learn to read it too. And this was brought about much sooner than you would have supposed it possible: for as Henry learned the Persian letters from day to day of Mr. Smith, he had been accustomed afterwards to write them on a slate, and make Boosy copy them as they sat together; and so by degrees he taught them all to his *bearer* before he was in possession of the Hindostannec copy of the chapters.

"Now, my boy," said Mr. Smith, "you are in the safe way of giving instruction in an ancient path cast up by God. Jeremiah 18:15. Do not trust to the words of your own wisdom, but to the word of God. Hold fast to the Scripture, dear boy, and you will be safe. And be not impatient if the seed you sow should not spring up immediately: something tells me I shall see Boosy a Christian before I die: or if I do not see that day, he that out-lives me will."

Now the time arrived when Henry's mamma was to leave

Calcutta. Indeed, she had stayed much longer there than she had at first proposed; but there were so many amusements going forward; so much gay company; so many fashionable dresses to purchase; that she could not find in her heart to leave them, although she was heartily tired of Mr. Smith's company. She respected him, indeed, as an old friend and worthy man; but he had such particular ways, she said, that sometimes she had difficulty to put up with them.

She proposed, as she went up the country, to stop at Berhampore, to see Mrs. Baron. When Henry heard of this he was greatly pleased, yet, when he came to take leave of Mr. Smith, he cried very much.

As they went up the river Henry took every opportunity of reading his chapters to his *bearer*, when his mamma could not overhear him: and he had many opportunities early in the morning, and in the afternoon when his mamma was asleep, as she always slept for an hour after *tiffin*. And he proceeded very well indeed, Boosy daily improving, at least in the knowledge of the Bible, till the weather suddenly becoming excessively hot, Henry was seized with a return of violent pain in his side, and other very bad symptoms. He became paler and thinner, and could not eat. His mamma, having no company to divert her, soon took notice of the change in the child, and began to be frightened; and so was his *bearer*. So they made all the haste they could to Berhampore, that they might procure advice from the doctors there, and get into a cool house; for the boat was excessively hot: but notwithstanding all the haste which they made, there was a great change in the poor little boy before they reached Berhampore.

When they were come within a day's journey of the place, they sent a servant forward to Mrs. Baron's; so that, when the *budgerow* anchored next day near the cantonments, Mrs. Baron herself was waiting on the shore with *palanquins* ready to carry them to her house. As soon as the board was fixed from the boat to the bank of the river, she jumped out of her *palanquin*, and was in the *budgerow* in a minute, with little Henry in her arms. "O my dear boy!" she said, "my dear, dear boy!" She could say no more, so great was her joy but when she looked at him and saw how very ill he appeared, her joy was presently damped; and she said, in her haste, to his mamma, "Dear madam, what is the matter with Henry? he looks very ill."

"Yes," said his mamma, "I am sorry to say that he is very ill: we must lose no time in getting advice for him."

"Do not cry, dear Mrs. Baron," said little Henry, seeing the tears running down her cheeks; "we must all die, you know we must, and death is very sweet to those who love the Lord Jesus Christ."

"O, my child," said his mamma, "why do you talk of dying? You will live to be a judge yet, and we shall see you with seven silver sticks before your *palanquin*."

"I do not wish it, mamma," said Henry.

The more Mrs. Baron looked at Henry, the more she was affected. For some moments she could not speak, or command her feelings at all: but after having drank a little water she became more composed, and proposed that they should all immediately remove to her house. And when she found herself shut up in her *palanquin*, she prayed earnestly to God, that whether the sweet babe lived or died, he might not be taken from her in this sickness: but that she might, with the help of God, administer holy nourishment to his immortal soul, and comfort to his little weak body.

When they were arrived at Mrs. Baron's house, she caused Henry to be laid on a sofa by day in the sitting-room, and at night in a room close by her own. The chief surgeon of the station was immediately sent for, and every thing was done for little Henry that the tenderest love could suggest.

Berhampore happened at that time to be very full; and Henry's mamma, finding many of her old acquaintance there, was presently so deeply engaged in paying and receiving visits, that she seemed again almost entirely to forget Henry, and all her concern about him: comforting herself, when she was going to a great dinner or ball, that Mrs. Baron would be with him, and he would be well taken care of. But it is a poor excuse to make for our neglect of duty, and one that I fear will not stand at the day of judgment, to say that there are others that will do it as well for us.

Notwithstanding all the surgeon could do, and all the care of Mrs. Baron, Henry's illness increased upon him; and every one had reason to think that the dear little fellow's time upon earth would soon come to an end. Mr. and Mrs. Baron were by turns his almost constant nurses; when one left him, the other generally took the place by his couch. It was very interesting to see a fine lively young man, like Mr. Baron, attending a little sick child; sometimes administering to him his food or medicine, and sometimes reading the Bible to him—but Mr. Baron feared God.

When Henry first came to Berhampore he was able to take the air in an evening in a *palanquin*, and could walk about the house; and two or three times he read a chapter in the Hindostannee Bible to Boosy: but he was soon too weak to read, and his airings became shorter and shorter. He was at last obliged to give them quite up, and to take entirely to his couch and bed, where he remained until his death.

When Boosy saw that his little *sahib's* end was drawing on, he was very sorrowful, and could hardly be persuaded to leave him night or day, even to get his *khauna*. He did every thing he could think of to please him, and more, as he afterwards said, to please his little dying master, than his God: he began to read his chapters with some diligence; and little Henry would lie on his couch, listening to Boosy as he read (imperfectly indeed) the word of God in Hindostannee. Often he would stop him to explain to him what he was reading; and very beautiful sometimes were the remarks which he made, and better suited to the understanding of his bearer than those of an older or more learned person would have been.

The last time that his *bearer* read to him, Mrs. Baron sitting by him, he suddenly stopped him, saying, "Ah, Boosy, if I had never read the *Bible*, and did not believe in it, what an unhappy creature should I now be for in a very short time I shall 'go down to the grave to come up no more;' Job 7:9; that is, until my body is raised at the last day. When I was out last, I saw a very pretty burying-ground with many trees about it. I knew that I should soon lie there; I mean that my body would: but I was not afraid, because I love my Lord Jesus Christ, and I know that he will go down with me unto the grave. I shall sleep with him, and 'I shall be satisfied when I awake with his likeness.'" Psalm 17:15. He then turned to Mrs. Baron, and said, "'I know that my Redeemer liveth, and that he shall stand at the latter day upon the earth; and though after my skin, worms destroy this body, yet in my flesh shall I see God.' Job 19:25–26. O kind Mrs. Baron! who, when I was a poor sinful child, brought me to the knowledge of my dear Redeemer; anointing me with sweet ointment (even his precious blood) for my burial, which was soon to follow."

"Dear child!" said Mrs. Baron, hardly able to preserve her composure, "dear child! give the glory to God!"

"Yes, I will glorify him for ever and ever," cried the poor little boy; and raised himself up in his couch, joining his small and taper fingers together: "yes, I will praise him, I will love him. I was a grievous sinner; every imagination of the thought of my heart was evil continually; I hated all good things; I hated even my Maker: but he sought me out; he washed me from my sins in his own blood; he gave me a new heart; he has clothed me with the garments of salvation, and hath put on me the robe of righteousness; he 'hath abolished death, and brought life and immortality to light.'" 2 Timothy 1:10. Then turning to his *bearer*, he said, "O my poor bearer! what will become of you 'if you neglect so great salvation?' " Hebrews 2:3. "O Lord Jesus Christ," he added, "turn the heart of my poor *bearer!*" This short prayer, which little Henry made in Hindostannee, his *bearer* repeated, scarcely knowing what he was doing. And this, as he afterwards told Mr. Smith, was the first prayer he had ever made to the true God—the first time he had ever called upon his holy name.

Having done speaking, little Henry laid his head down on his pillow, and closed his eyes. His spirit was full of joy indeed, but his flesh was weak; and he lay some hours in a kind of slumber. When he awoke he called Mrs. Baron, and begged her to sing the verse of the hymn he loved so much,

"Jesus sought me," etc.

which she had taught him at Dinapore. He smiled while she was singing, but did not speak.

The same evening, Boosy being left alone with his little master, and seeing that he was wakeful and inclined to talk, said, "I have been thinking all day that I am a sinner, and always have been one; and I begin to believe that my sins are such as Gunga cannot wash away. I wish I could believe in the Lord Jesus Christ!"

When Henry heard this he strove to raise himself up, but

was unable, on account of his extreme weakness; yet his eyes sparkled with joy: he endeavored to speak, but could not; and at last he burst into tears. He soon, however, became more composed, and pointing to his *bearer* to sit down on the floor by his couch, he said, "Boosy, what you have now said makes me very happy: I am very, very happy to hear you call yourself a sinner, and such an one as Gunga cannot make clean. It is Jesus Christ who has made this known to you: he has called you to come unto him. Faithful is he that calleth you. I shall yet see you, my poor *bearer*, 'in the general assembly and church of the first born.' Hebrews 12:23. You were kind to me when my own father and mother were dead. The first thing I can remember, is being carried by you to the *Mangoe tope,* near my mamma's house at Patna. Nobody loved me then but you: and could I depart in peace and leave you behind me in the way to hell? I could not bear to think of it! Thank God! I knew he would hear my prayer; but I thought that perhaps you would not begin to become a Christian till I was gone. When I am dead, Boosy," added the little boy, "do you go to Mr. Smith at Calcutta. I cannot write to him, or else I would; but you shall take him one lock of my hair (I will get Mrs. Baron to cut it off and put it in a paper) and tell him that I sent it. You must say that Henry L——, that died at Berhampore, sent it with this request, that good Mr. Smith would take care of his poor *bearer*, when he has lost *caste* for becoming a Christian." Boosy would have told Henry that he was not quite determined to be a Christian, and that he could not think of losing *caste;* but Henry, guessing what he was going to say, put his hand upon his mouth. "Stop! stop!" he said: "do not say words which will make God angry, and which you will be sorry for by and by: for I know you will die a Christian. God has begun a good work in you, and I am certain that he will finish it."

While Henry was talking to his *bearer*, Mrs. Baron had come into the room: but, not wishing to interrupt him, she had stood behind his couch; but now she came forward. As soon as he saw her, he begged her to take off his cap, and cut off some of his hair, as several of his friends wished for some. She thought that she would endeavor to comply with his request. But when she took off his cap, and his beautiful hair fell about his pale, sweet face; when she considered how soon the time would be when the eye that hath seen him shall see him no more; she could not restrain her feelings; but throwing down the scissors, and putting her arm around him, "O my child! my dear, dear child!" she said, "I cannot bear it! I cannot part with you yet!"

The poor little boy was affected: but he gently reproved her, saying, "'If you love me you will rejoice because I go to my Father.'" John 14:28.

There was a considerable change in the child during the night: and all the next day till evening he lay in a kind of slumber: and when he was roused to take his medicine or nourishment, he seemed not to know where he was, or who was with him. In the evening he suddenly revived, and asked for his mamma. He had seldom asked for her before. She was in the house, for she was not so hard-hearted (thoughtless as she was) as to go into gay company at this time, when the child's death might be hourly expected. She trembled much when she heard that he asked for her. She was conscious, perhaps, that she had not fulfilled her duty to him. He received her affectionately when she went up to his bedside, and begged that everybody would go out of the room, saying that he had something very particular to speak about to her. He talked to her for some time, but nobody knows the particulars of their conversation: though it is believed that the care of her immortal soul was the subject of the last discourse which this dear little boy held with her. She came out of his room with her eyes swelled with crying, and his little well-worn Bible in her hand, (which he had probably given her, as it always lay on the bed by him,) and shutting herself in her room, she remained without seeing any one, till the news was brought that all was over. From that time she never gave her mind so entirely to the world as she had formerly done; but became a more serious character, and daily read little Henry's Bible.

But now to return to little Henry. As there are but few persons who love to meditate upon the scenes of death, and too many are only able to view the gloomy side of them, instead of following, by the eye of faith, the glorious progress of the departing saint, I will hasten to the end of my story. The next day at twelve o'clock, being Sunday, he was delivered from this evil world, and received into glory. His passage was calm, although not without some mortal pangs. "May we die the death of the righteous, and may our last end be like his." Numbers 23:10.

Mr. and Mrs. Baron and his *bearer* attended him to the last moment, and Mr. Baron followed him to the grave.

Sometime after his death his mamma caused a monument to be built over his grave, on which was inscribed his name, Henry L——, and his age, which at the time of his death was eight years and seven months. Underneath was a part of his favorite verse from 1 Thessalonians 5, altering only one word; "Faithful is he that called *me.*" And afterwards was added, by desire of Mr. Smith, this verse from James 5:20. "He which converteth a sinner from the error of his way, shall save a soul from death, and shall hide a multitude of sins."

When I first visited Berhampore, I went to see little Henry's monument. It was then white and fair, and the inscription very plain; but I am told that the damp of the climate has so defaced the inscription, and blackened the whole monument, that it cannot be distinguished from the tombs which surround it. But

this is of little consequence, as all who remember Henry L——
have long ago left Berhampore; and we are assured, that this dear
child has himself received "an inheritance that fadeth not away."
1 Peter 1:4. "The world passeth away, and the lust thereof: but
he that doeth the will of God abideth for ever." 1 John 2:17.

Every person who reads this story will, I think, be anxious
to know what became of Boosy. Immediately after the funeral
of his little *sahib*, having received his wages, with a handsome
present, he carried the lock of hair, which Mrs. Baron sealed up
carefully, with a letter from her to Mr. Smith. He was received
into Mr. Smith's family, and removed with him to a distant part
of India; where, shortly after, he renounced *caste*, and declared
himself a Christian. After due examination, he was baptized;
and continued till his death (which happened not long after)
a sincere Christian. It was on the occasion of the baptism of
Boosy, to whom the Christian name of John was given, that the
last verse was added to the monument of little Henry.

From Mrs. Baron and Mr. Smith I gathered most of the
anecdotes relative to the history of Henry L——.

Little children in India, remember Henry L——, and "go
and do likewise." Luke 10:37. For "they that be wise shall shine
as the brightness of the firmament; and they that turn many to
righteousness, as the stars for ever and ever." Daniel 12:3.

———

LITTLE CHILDREN IN AMERICA,—Think on Henry L——,
and *go and do likewise*. He was born among ignorant heathen,
those who worshipped the rivers, the stones, and the images
they had made. You live in a Christian land, where the true
God, he who dwells in the heavens, and who knows every thing
you say and do, is adored. Little Henry was an orphan; he had

a kind friend to watch over and protect him; a compassionate stranger informed him about religion and the way to heaven, and gave him a Bible, the book of God. You have parents and instructors to tell you of right and wrong, how to love God and keep his commandments, and you are early taught to read his word. Did, then, this little child hearken to what was told him, and read God's holy book? Did he strive also to cause his poor bearer to leave his false gods and turn from them to love and serve the one only true God? When, therefore, your parents and friends would restrain you from what is wrong, and prompt you to the exercise of what is right; when they would urge upon you the necessity of religion, and of reading that book which contains the words of eternal life; or whensoever you yourselves have an opportunity of reproving others around you, who are living without God in the world, and who regard not his holy commandments, think how Henry L—— would have done, and *go and do likewise.*

My young friends, Henry was only one of the many destitute children in that heathen land. Thousands are there now, who have no kind lady to instruct them, and who, I fear, will never be thus favored, and hear of Christ and God. You perceive what pleasure it gave him to be told of these things, and how glad he was to receive a Bible. Think what he would have done, and how dreadful must have been his situation, when sick and dying, had he not met with the compassionate lady.

Now you have heard of *Missionaries.* These are pious and benevolent persons, who leave their beloved friends and their native shores to go to those distant countries, and carry Bibles to such poor children as little Henry, and tell them about religion. Should you not like to send a Bible to those destitute children? or to do something to let them know there is a God? Suppose you were in little Henry's country, and some kind persons should send one to instruct you and bring you good books; would you not feel very grateful to them?

You are small now, and much is not to be expected of you. But remember, should every one do but little, yet, in the whole, much would be done. There are those who are willing to leave their country to make known to the heathen the existence of God, and the way of salvation by his Son Jesus Christ, and convey to them his holy word; and they wait only for means to enable them to go. Let then every one, who, in reading this little Tract, felt pity toward Henry in his forsaken state, and rejoiced when he found a friend to instruct and comfort him, do something toward sending them.

Remember also, dear children, that although you are now young and dependant upon others, you are daily growing older. Your parents and your friends will soon be gone, and you will stand in their places; property will be at your disposal, and you will have the direction of whatever concerns the church and your country. In after life, therefore, whenever any measure is proposed for the benefit of the heathen; whenever your assistance is asked to promote in any way this important cause, think how little Henry L—— of Dinapore would have done, and *go and do likewise.* Verily, I say unto you, you shall not lose your reward.

www.ingramcontent.com/pod-product-compliance
Lightning Source LLC
Chambersburg PA
CBHW020443030426
42337CB00014B/1364